UNAVAILABLE

UNAVAILABLE

GINA M. SMALLWOOD
TRUE RENAISSANCE ENTERPRISE

Unavailable/Available

Printed in the United States of America

First Printing, 2018

ISBN 978-0-9993157-5-0

True Renaissance Enterprise, LLC
GSmallwoodsmiles@gmail.com

www.TrueRenaissance.net

To every living being that has suffered abuse
May you heal and recover
Knowing you are a significant contribution to
universal peace

As wisdom spoke truth
The devil would always say
"You sure are one of the most sapient"

Wisdom in a whisper
Chuckling along with Grace

It is not I
To whom
The Glory belongs
It is God
The unseen face

Cuz if it were I alone
To deal with you on my own
I woulda
removed your evil ass
A long time ago

CONTENTS

CONTENTS

CONTENTS

This is a story about a little girl who longed for the love she desperately sought from her father. She thought love was somewhere on a pedestal. With each aching episode of her life, she continued seeking false hope in a man's approval, affection, and lust.

The irony is the more she tried to free herself, the more imprisoned she became. The price she paid was staggering, as was the toll it took on her spirit. From each failed relationship, she carried fuel that added to the fire of her desire for someone else to love her. Each flame nearly engulfed her dwindling candle, almost extinguishing it to a deadly halt.

As she begins to express her emotions, she discovers just how much she feared and that she was the roadblock to her authentic self. She discovers that the love she sought was not something to seek. She realizes that the power of self-love is within, a birthright, God's gift to every being. Self-love unrecognized is a strong magnet that attracts others who lack self-love.

Unavailable is her journey through poetry, letters, prose and quotes; what she tried to hide would eventually unfold, unveiling itself, bringing with it all the emotional baggage filled with insecurities and a mirrored image of her brokenness.

"The person who tells you to trust them the most
Is the person who has the potential to hurt you the most"

CHAPTER ONE - FEAR

Future

Expectations

Aren't

Realized

No longer a necessary chapter

PROVEN

It is scientifically proven that continued physical
and/or mental abuse can cause the human brain to
suffer many psychological disorders. Anticipatory
Anxiety happens to be one of them, which stems from
an abundance of harsh, traumatic, negative and painful
events. Although life includes ebbs and flows,
someone who suffers from this disorder can get stuck
in the lows and become victim to its blows.

HELLO HELLO HELLO

I can't see or hear you
Excuse Me
I'm busy trying to find myself

"Hey sexy, Damn sexy"

Okay
Now you've got my attention

BAIT

I was easy bait for broken males

One slick word and

they had pulled my coattail

"Sexy" was the word of choice

that I loved to hear

Hell I exuded it

with every outfit

hairstyle

eyeliner

and lip-gloss

I would wear

It was so easy to lure me into feeling

what I thought

was compassion for a sick friend

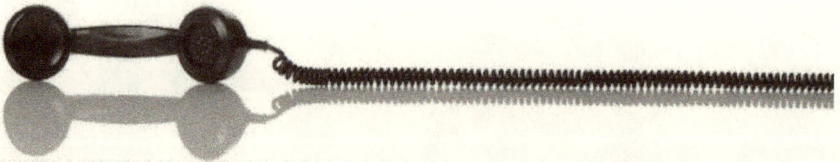

HELLO HELLO HELLO

I know I'm all jacked up

Can you

Someone

Anyone

Please

Help me out of this mess

Sure that's what my daddy taught me

and

"Father knows best"

EXCUSE ME EXCUSE ME

Did you just lie to me and confess love

Confusing my heart

Into thinking

What was spoken

Would be your actions

Cuz you wanted to taste my stuff

COOKIES CRUMBLED

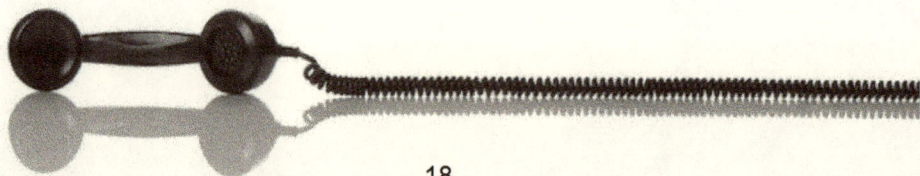

COME AND PLAY

Inside this ocean of birth

Tell me Mister

What is your worth

Can you provide

Basic necessities

Or are you just selling pipe dreams

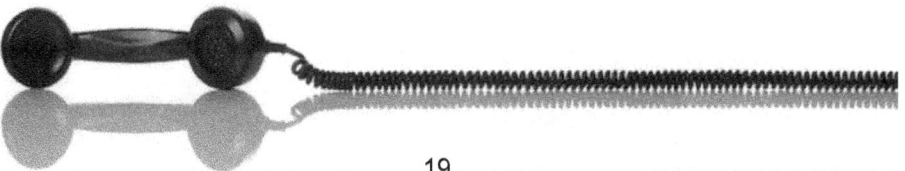

DON'T MAKE ME ANY PROMISES
AND
I PROMISE I WON'T HOLD YOU
ACCOUNTABLE

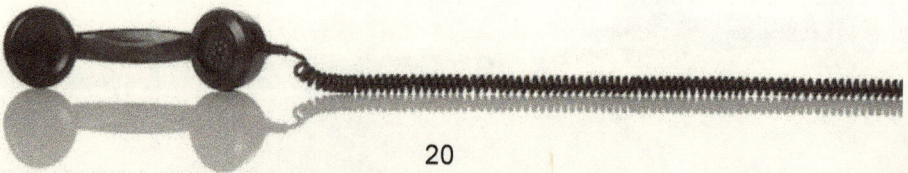

Slam

"Damn"

I just hit the floor

Didn't you promise that shit wouldn't
happen anymore

QUEEN/BITCH

You queen

YOU FUCKING BITCH

The father

The cycle

Part of the script

Of all this madness

I believed

I was stuck in

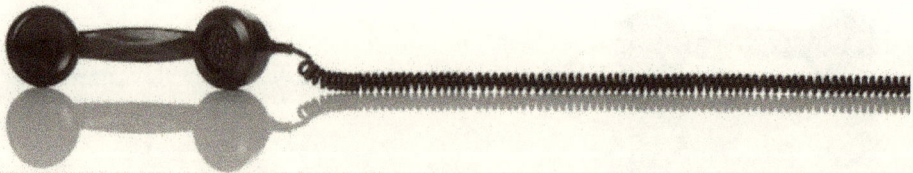

Dis Dis

You've always shown me who you were
With the utmost dis and dis respect
I thought I knew your caliber
Torch her
Was a familiar place
I'd learned this
Long before you entered this space
This brutality
I wanted it to make some sense
I'd become accustomed to it
Making dis and dis my fault
Being happy when I was treated nice
Sad and alone when dis dis appeared
Codependency
My best friend
She loves sorrow
Hey let me in
I want another round tomorrow
Of dis here shit
Valley low
Dis dis appointment
Here we go

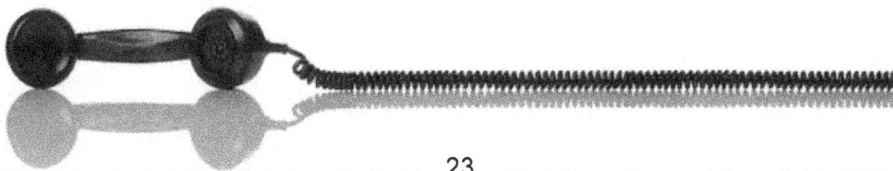

LOADED SHOTGUN

COCKED
It's at my head
Lord/Lady God
Is this my time to go
Screaming
Praying
For your help
Evil
Loud and clear
"Fuck God
He ain't here"
Ring Ring
Doorbell
It's you
Disguised as a lamb
Friend
Loaded Glock
In a sock
Is everything okay
As evil shook behind the door
Showing its coward face
Answering yes
And slowly walking away

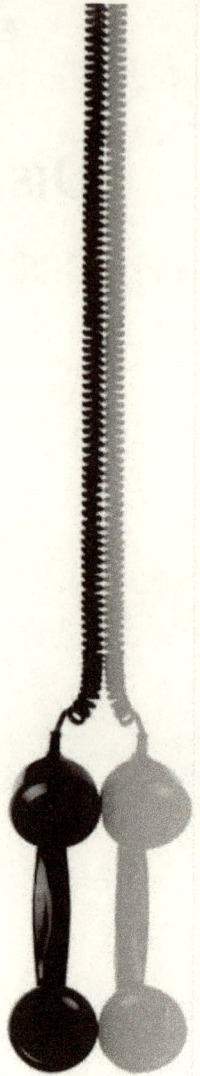

Venom

That would be the charm

It warps me every time

In his voice

The tone of hopelessness

Always pulls me in

It's soft and subtle

Sweet as tupelo honey

Like it would never do any harm

But as soon as love gets too close

It bites you with delight

Poisonous And

Slithers away

YET WITH THE FORECAST OF
TSUNAMIS
TORNADOES
AND
HURRICANES

I'VE FALLEN
Off
The Wagon
Again

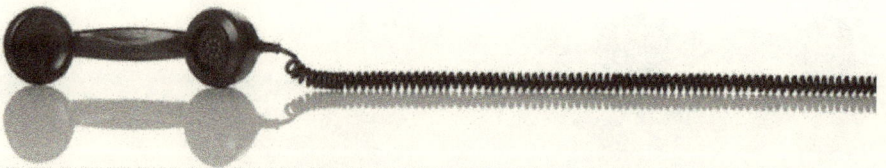

Unavailable

+

Unavailable

=

TOXIC

INTOXICATED

Whew...
Overcome by seduction
All the pain just went away
From the moment I read his words
I was led astray
Each text message pulling me in
The comfort of insanity was about to begin
Hell, when the phone rang and
I heard his voice
My soul left yearning
I easily surrendered
I had no other choice
I've got to see you even it's the last time
For what could happen in one night
I stood the chance of losing my mind
I approached this evening
With what we would share
With all love
No flame
No flare
As you opened the door
Watching from a distance
I gave you my heart with no resistance.

When you asked me if I would like a drink
My response was invigorating
I jumped on this ship
With no thoughts of sinking
So I drank from the glass more than once
Imagining the taste of what we once had
As I began to share
Poetry and wisdom
You showed signs disguised as care
As I began to lie in comfort
You smiled and stated
"You're teasing me
Let's go upstairs"
Guiding me to a familiar sanctuary
Kissing me in all the right places
I slowly slipped out of my fear
And a year of celibacy
Turning into butter
Surrendering to your will
You had
Completely
Intoxicated me

PAIN FOR FUN

MEET ME IN A CITY

WHERE YOU GET TO SHOW YOURSELF

I PROMISE I'LL BE GOOD TO YOU AND PUT YOU ON
A SHELF

MEET YOU AT THE AIRPORT

WITH FLOWERS AND ALL

GREET YOU WITH A BIG HUG

TENDER KISS

DRIVE YOU TO THE BALL

MAKE LOVE TO YOU

BUT AS SOON AS YOU SHOW SIGNS OF NEEDING
ME

I'LL KICK YOU TO THE CURB

CLOSING THE DOOR

LEAVING YOU WANTING MORE

EMOTIONALLY

I felt sorrow

I felt anger

I felt hurt

I felt stupid

I felt rejection

I felt disrespected

I felt disappointment

I felt isolation

I felt loneliness

I felt fear

And still fought back the tears

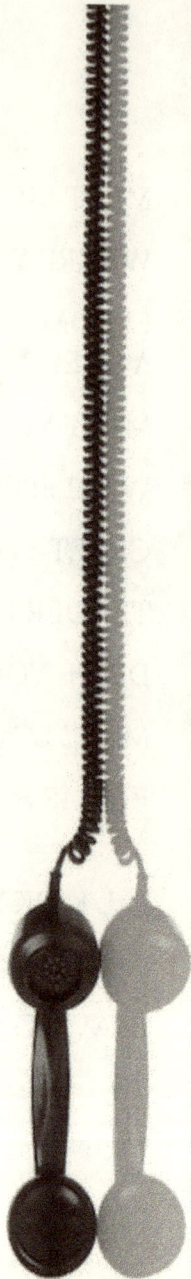

RED CARPET

How many times can you take a ride on
                    THIS HERE DIRTY SHIT

Skating

Hoping

Praying

One day it's gonna get clean

Acting like you some
Human cleaning machine

Wake up Sister
You been living in a dream

With a forecast
Cloudy skies
No sun in sight

Years of overwhelming strife
Thinking you can change
The dirt and the grit

Girl
Simply put
                  THIS AIN'T YO SHIT

Still
You allow them fibers
Keep hitting you in yo face
Smacking you all around the place

Acting like you ain't got nothing in your soul
Looking for someone to take control

How insecure can you be

The nitty gritty
No matter how kind
And clean you think you may be

If you don't learn to stand up
And love yourself
You will continue to be
On this dirty
Red carpet ride

U

C

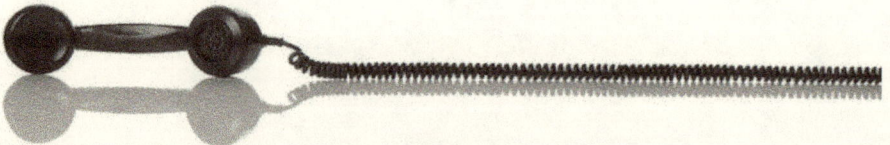

FABRICATE

Our lives somehow don't tell the truth
We get lost in wanting to feel good
Even if it means suppressing where we failed
Hiding behind false pretenses
Until we don't know ourselves
We become what others want us to be
Believing peace means silence
All the while being
Misleading
Feeding a reality that's not real
Continuing to misplace
And
Fabricate ideals

THE ADDICT

He promises me the moon and sky
Especially when that motherfucker's high

     I I I I I I'm coming over to see you Boo
       Cuz all the things I promised
        I'm ready to give to you

 What you doing
He always ask
Like I'm stepping out on him
When the truth is he never really stepped in

      You already know the other woman
        She's a drug and
       She damn sure ain't your friend

He's always blocking my groove
Holding me down to my every move
Cuz he knows when I'm away
I just might find a pleasurable place to stay

     He wants me in a space under his control
    With broken dreams and love for his main girl
      Whose name ain't yours by the way
    It's a powdered substance the color of a pearl

Damn I say over and over to myself
Why do I keep putting up with all this strife
Somehow in my mind I believe
I can love him into a better life

I keep fooling myself
Hoping Wishing Praying
I will one day have the courage to say

Sweetie your addiction is more powerful than us
And without God and treatment
Your life will continue to be in disarray

Meanwhile I battle with myself
Because my heart and spirit have learned
To accept pain and trauma as a part of love

As I come to a realization
It is not just my man who is addicted
It is me too who has major issues
When it comes down to facing the truth

So before I point the finger using love as an excuse
I need to take a closer look at myself
And figure out why my fear of being alone is the real noose

I've played the role as an enabler long enough
It's time I stopped using my man's addiction
as an escape and
Face my own addictive behavior in its place

The Greatest Fear
is that
of being alone....

YOU AND HE AND HE

I wanted you and he and he
To want me

Please want me
For me
Let me show you all of me
Please want me for me

I wanted you and he and he
To want me

Let me give you every chance to want me
Let me show you just what you got
cuz

I wanted you and he and he
To want me

Open my legs wide
Come on in
Meet my soul
A place for me to hold
You in my heart

I wanted you and he and he
To want me

A beggar can't be choosy
When one is blind to self
Lost instead
Seeking value in someone else
Placing conditions that don't exist
Wanting power that was stolen
Given away
Stuck in shock

Waiting

No

Know

Waking

I

Waking

Want

Waking

Me

Waking

And

Waking

Me

Waking

For

Awake

Me!

WHEN YOU LIVE
IN TRUTH

There is no room for fear

For All the people in an abusive or toxic relationship

Write a list: **Why?**

Now share this with a therapist!

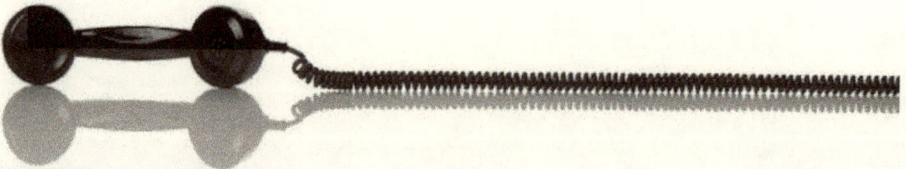

CHAPTER TWO - PAIN

Perpetual

Anxiety

Internalized

Negativity

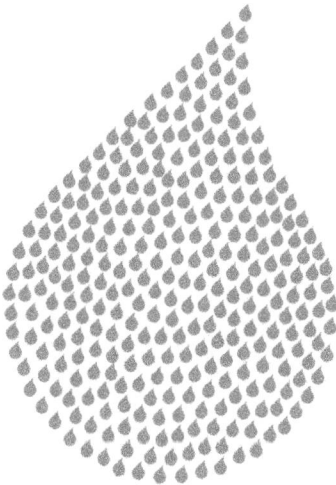

The Human Experience Chapter

WHAT DID I DO

For you to treat me so mean

I'm not liking the pain

I feel like I'm bleeding from the spleen

Please look at me

Tell me the truth

Cuz your actions

Are contradictions

From the words you spoke

Foolishly I believed you...

Leave me be

Finally

I'm free

"THE SCRIPT"

I learned as a daughter to find
happiness in misery and sorrow

Now I understand why I allowed you

in my life

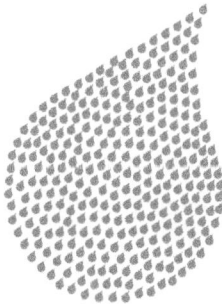

MY BAD

My fault

I took the rejection you gave personal

Causing unnecessary pain and suffering

I died a few times stumbling over the same

Hard as stone

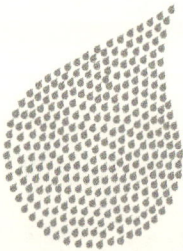

I'D YET GOT MYSELF INTO A TWISTED SITUATION

CLOUDY

I
I
I
Couldn't see myself
I had no clue
I was in a web
Where being in this relationship was more about
Feeding the need to feel someone else's pain
I'd become the savior of sorrow
Yet again
Confusion followed
I didn't want to face this truth
You never really wanted me
I was just one to feed your need
Greedy ass appetite
Stuck like so many other trees
I couldn't see the light
Till the pain of the need
Almost took all that I had away from me
Including my life

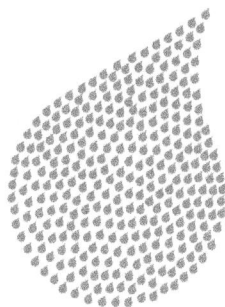

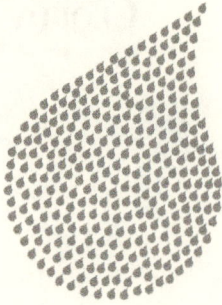

DADDY TOLD ME

To do everything with God in it

I wonder if every time he punched me in the face

God was in his fist

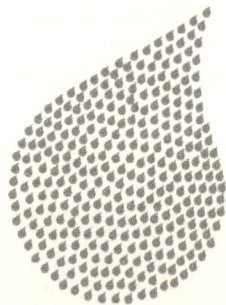

THE SINS OF A FATHER

It is said:

"The sins of a Father are passed to his sons"

And the gun my son used

Was the gun I thought I needed to protect me

From you

And the gun you used

Was the gun you bought me to protect me

From my father

Daddy

I'm not your son I'm your daughter

HEY DADDY

I'M COMING HOME TODAY

"BE CAREFUL

TODAY IS THE DAY
I WAS SHOT
AND BLINDED

40 YEARS AGO"

WOW

It's been 40 years I suffered so
Not knowing this Anniversary
Would bring such
A blow

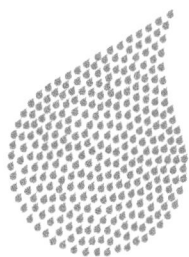

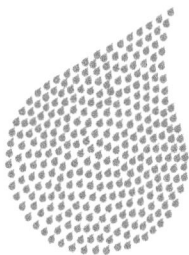

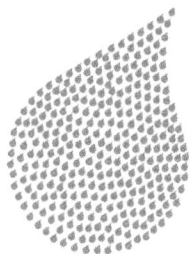

BANG

One shot to the head

All this negativity

Rendered

Surrender

My only child is dead

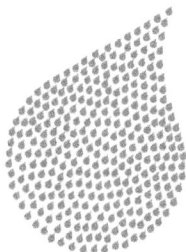

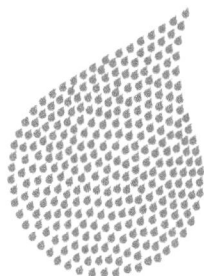

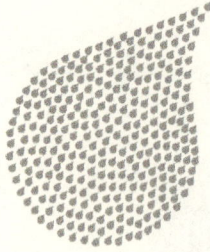

Trying not to disappoint God

For I know God is with me

Still, I feel so all alone

All that I've worked so hard for has shattered

Like glass broken by a stone

Surviving suicide has left me so displaced

When I look in the mirror

I don't even see my face

As I try to pick up the pieces

Using all the strength I have

I become motionless

From the memories of the past

No matter what I do or where I go

Everything is moving slow

It's hard to keep the faith in things I don't know

I keep praying and asking God to help me through

If the light does not soon appear

I'll be left without a clue

I'm at a crossroad with nothing else to do

DEATH I WANTED ITS FACE

Even started my car in a garage

Trying to get to that place

Pop no more silence

Shook me to my core

I could not go through with it

There had to be another door

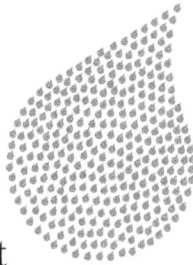

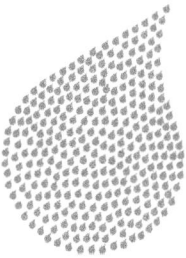

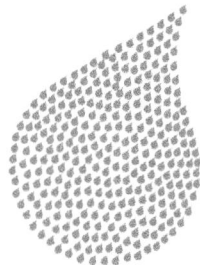

MOSES

Is what my Daddy called me after my son's death
"Kelvin was your bridge over troubled water"
That was months after he blamed me
In his normal rage
Yet another blow
I stood frozen
Having to be carried
Back to the front door
It wasn't until that moment
The marriage that ended in a violent divorce
Felt the pain of my script
Apologetic for all that he had done
Bringing harm to my spirit
And with a clear statement
"If either of my parents ever spoke to me with such brutality
I would shoot them to take them out of their misery"

"Daughter
You still have time to get your life in order"

I SUFFERED SILENTLY

Tears flowed

Stained sheets

Salt water

No one can swim

Float

In this Dead Sea

In

Mosaic

Gray

Clear

Provoking thoughts

Change color

Slight breeze

Deep waters

Carry me

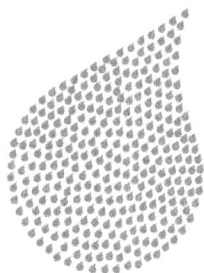

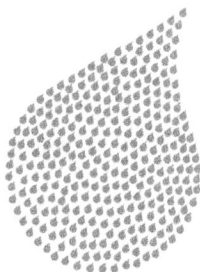

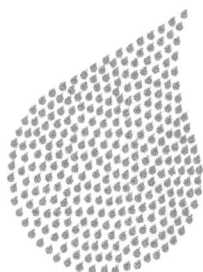

FALSE PHALLUS

I somehow found it difficult to get through
The dream of tattooing a cross on my back
As I pondered what the message meant
This lifetime I would wear
Still not comprehending
All this in my head
Over and over
I found it hard to forgive myself
For loving being in pain with you more than anything else
The message in this dream
Delivered some years ago
Prompted me to ask my son to treat me to this artwork
I would display
He chuckled "Sure Mom
I'll gift you this
It's May the month of Mother's Day"

...And it would be his last!

Not knowing the significance or
How it related to the mess I was in
The love I was directing wasn't yours to receive
Instead it should have been directed to my son
Who I now know was in dire need
Warned by many
Be careful in the waters that you tread
You only have one child
Don't be lead astray
So the tattoo I wear on my back is a constant
reminder of the cross I bear
Heavy weighted in sadness
Over the passing of my beautiful son
Whose love was lost in translation
to an unworthy one

I STOPPED CRYING

I stopped crying
Cuz I didn't want to feel the pain
Fearful of filling
Rivers swollen
Drown the earth
My cup runneth over
Suppress my total being
Vulnerable
Delicate little pearl
Somewhere
You got lost
Dealing with this world
Taking insecurities
Blanket
Keep me warm
There's so much I missed
Being Daddy's little girl

SLOWLY

I stepped

I crept

Turned into a ghost

Filling my fragile spirit

With some of the same host

Ten, twenty, forty years how can this be

You still kicked me

Down a steeper hill

Breathless

Air

I breathe

Thank God

For mercy on me

Beware:

CHARM

Can be venomous

Especially

If it comes from an insecure person

ONCE AGAIN

You lured me with sugar
Then threw salt into my wounds
I can't blame you completely
I already knew who you were
A wolf in sheep's clothing
Nonetheless
I let you in
Once again
I guess I'd not learned my lesson
When it came to you
Forgetting the hurt
Year in and year out
Leaving me in such disillusionment
Taking one step forward
And two steps back
I lost all my mathematical abilities
Trying to multiply
Wishing the pain and drama with you would come back
I continued to try and figure out
This equation
One minus you still equals one
Searching for the root of the cause and
What this dysfunction was all about
Finally accepting it was never mine
It was just some deep-rooted shit
That needed
To fall off like leaves
Fall off an oak tree

WHY EVEN

Afraid

Ashamed

Dirty

Inadequate

Unfulfilled

Why even try

to be intimate with someone

who doesn't tell the truth

Hard Pill to swallow

Strike a pose
Lights
Camera
Re
Action
Thought I was the one
Years later
Still undone
Always been what he needed
Not completely what he wanted
Finally facing fear
Being all alone
Without the fantasy
Fairytale
Dream
Stumbling through wide awake
No more self -inflicted pain
Expecting anything that I can't
Give and receive in return
Has been a hard pill to swallow
A life lesson well learned

BUST A CAP

A nut

In my gut

What kinda

Abuse is that

To my womb

You must be true

Or else

I'll be carrying scars

Singing the blues

Raising a child

Who's jacked up just like you

DRAGGED

Ride or Die
I ain't no woman who lacks virtue
Not for a minute
Kinda trick
Trying to ride your magic carpet
I've been through shit you can't even pocket
Rosy is a color I've been trying to see
Since you've been in my life that color has decreased
I use to tell myself love him enough he'll change
That's the stupid hope
Like I'm on some kinda dope
Some people are ride or die
And some you have to get off the ride or die
I'm choosing to live
Not stumble over and over again
Freeing myself and letting go
Like the wind
That narcissistic being I so loved
I have to say goodbye
Or be dragged and lose my own damn life

I FIND THE EGO SELF

Getting stuck in the pain of disbelief

How could I possibly have believed a relationship
lacking integrity

Could ever have sanity

Silly girl

You can't water dirt without a seed and

Hope for a flower to grow

I DIED A MILLION TIMES
LOVING YOU

Hell
I no longer fear death
Climbed mountains and
lost my breath

I was once her

Your trophy that is

Like so many others

I lived off of the penis dream

As much as I wanted to be a wife

There was too much hell and too much strife

Congratulations I hope you find the one

My hopes for her

Are that you love her more

Than you love the drugs

Otherwise, she'll soon learn

What life can be with you

True misery

You can't run back to me

Cuz you've run over me

Killed me with your mess

I'm splattered on the pavement

Like roadkill

Left for birds to feed

Wrapping my arms around this cartilage

I peel myself

Up from the ground

I'm going to paste love in the sky

In front of heaven's gate

And wait to return

To the place

I was born

Leaving no remnants of ever being scorned

LAST CALL

So here I go
Shit, he offered housing
While I was stressed
I'm clear as daylight
He wants something else

For me
It's Redemption Mother-Fucker
A lifetime lesson I've already learned
Don't get caught up
In his misery
I tell myself

As I slowly reminisce on the past
Feeling a little sorrow for his high ass
Then I remember the pain
He's still selfish
Don't get caught up in his shit

He ain't been feeling well
For quite some time
It's habitual
You had to see it again to believe it
Several times with your own eyes

Not much has changed
Even with God
Showing him light
He's still playing
The same games

Now his heart
Is showing signs
Of abuse
He's taking several different pills
For his health and over use

Ignoring all the prevention
that could extend his life
Talking with his family members
about disability
a wealth they know all too well

The peace speaks
like a whisper
forest from a tree
this is a state of emergency

Flash warning   **this pathology is way too deep**

When it comes to mental health
watching your own behavior
seeing how you feel
is the first step
in loving yourself
and
recovering
from mental ills

Adios
Time to go
Check into a hotel

This round
This Last Call
for dysfunction to feed my pain
No longer serves a purpose in my brain

CHAPTER THREE - RELEASE

Remove

Expectations

Leaving

Ecstasy

Allowing

Sweetness

Entirely

Death comes in threes

You cannot build a bridge
unless
you are willing
to go through
the water

VICTIM I ZED

Picking
Up
Myself
Every emotion
Every tear
The fear
Through all these years
Looking not just for you
But my daddy left me without a clue
This emptiness
Has left me breathless
Melodrama
Come on in
Let me take care of you
My friend
The blindness
My heart trained
To work on other people's pain
Hiding
Parts
Leaving me
Yet
Empty

Every time
I want to feel her
I freeze
Perplexity
She frightens me
Every emotion
Every tear
Letting go
Lost
Control
On my knees
With
No other place to go
But in the arms
Of
This space to be
On a ledge
Learning
Yearning
Out of Stillness
The necessity
To Care
With
For
Is
About Me

No

Excuse
For
Abuse!

Daddy

Your brutality broke me into pieces

The remnants of our relationship left me

Shattered

Scattered

Shards

Cutting

Into

My life

As I pick of the sharp pieces

One by One

Putting myself back together

I realize

I am love

HOW DO YOU SAY GOODBYE?

When the truth is you never said hello!

I MUST LET GO

of why I was with them

Hold on to why I left them

Return to who I was before I ever met them

B GROWN

If someone doesn't show you respect

Kick their ass to the curb

Even if you standing on the corner trying to survive

Know you will be kept alive

Don't lose sleep trying to collect peace

Time is a resource you can't gain back

And wasting it on someone who doesn't give a fuck

about you is simply whack

Even if it's in your heart to extend yourself

Don't ever devalue your personal wealth

Keep on Keeping on

Extending and reaching that validation for self

SCENT OF A MAN

Um Damn
Um Damn

Feminine meets Masculine
I'm melting inside your smell

Pheromones
Unseen
Felt

Chills
Comfort
Know
No
What is this?

Fool Me
Lost Concentration
Betrayal

Warmth
Hocus Pocus
Focus Focus
Girl, it's not his essence
It's Just … His Damn Scent!

THIN LINE BETWEEN NEED AND WANT

I somehow thought I needed you

But as I begin to step away

I clearly begin to see the truth

Love is what I needed

But my need to feel wanted

Blocked the view

HE ONLY WANTED

Me for pleasure

He only needed me

For everything

WANTING SOMETHING YOU DON'T HAVE

Is no different than

Having something you don't want

TRYING TO BE ENOUGH

I somehow got stuck

On trying to be

Enough woman for you

Then the realization set in

It was not

I was never enough

It was

I was always too much.

GOODBYE

Dear Person of Disinterest,

It's evident that you never respected me,
which really isn't the issue. The issue is I
allowed you to disrespect me. As I draw to
the anniversary of meeting you, I'm
stopping the codependent behavior that has
ripped me apart. You're not the only person
I've been codependent with Darling but you
are the last!

Over and over again

Embedded in me

It was somehow my fault

I started to believe

I caused the bad

Accepting your criticism

Blinded by its hold

Switch turned off

Then on

Codependency

My best friend

I have to let you go

Little Trinket

Collecting dust

This past behavior

I must never trust

I CAN

I sometimes find myself

Missing

Parts

Of you

The parts that spoiled me

But

For all

The hell

I went through

I can spoil my damn self

FLASHBACK

Write what I'm feeling
Send it to your ass
A flashback from the past

Why would I want to experience whiplash

Shows me you're stuck in a place and time
Still numbing your feelings
From all the hurt
Forgiven by others
Deep waters
Still haven't learned to swim
Major issues
Management
Control
Inability to let go

Rehab
Is where you should Be

Instead you seek flashbacks from me

What the Fuck

Resonates

Wow
Many blessings
Come and go
As you continue
Seeking a high
Only found in sobriety

A freedom
To feel
Your pain
Riding it like the wind
Difficult to achieve
Not seeking anything

Knowing love seeks nothing in return
And gives abundantly

Sorry my friend
I'll keep you in prayer
With an understanding
There will be no flashbacks from me

FIRE

Is fire

You can play with it if you want to

I just hope you can deal with 3rd degree burns

SQUARE PEG

Sometimes in life we try to force a square peg

Into a round hole

If it doesn't fit

Let that shit

Go

REMEMBER

You broke up with him

because God knew

Your heart deserves the best

Remember that shit

and hold it

like a soft fluffy pillow

I FIND I AM HAPPY Now

With all of me

Than I was with parts of you

Taking any person's abusive behavior as something you caused starts the cycle. There may be things you love about a person that keep you entangled but as soon as their behavior is morally and emotionally compromising,

CHECK YOURSELF

BE KIND

Or

be gone

IF I DIE WITH JUST ONE FRIEND

I die a rich woman

If I die with many superficial friends

I die a broke ass chick

Dark Cloud

As tears roll down my face, the memories of my child cannot be replaced.

There are words to describe when a child's parents have died and when a spouse loses their groom or bride, orphan or widow is what we use to bring empathy and sympathy to that kind of pain a person goes through.

When a child dies from a tragic death like that of suicide, the word or name to describe parents left behind is survivor. The one who carries the spirit of their child, lingering memories, and an indescribable pain that sometimes can be so dark, you feel like you are going insane. I understand the term survive as this has become part of my life, knowing I carried my son from the womb to his tomb has sometimes brought me strife.

To all the mothers whose children have died tragically remember to go gently on yourself when that dark cloud appears bringing with it an insurmountable flow of tears, sometimes a sadness covered in strength and a lack of understanding from others who will never know pain this intense. Pat yourself on the back for each moment that you live. Know that while you may feel alone when the pain cuts deep, kicks you, and knocks you off your feet, there are numerous mothers both near and far whose lives have been affected leaving that dark cloud that permanent scar.

QUESTION AND ANSWER

With acceptance

It is just what it is

With un-acceptance

It becomes unjust

It becomes the question

Why

And you become the answer

The victim

How could you

      That would be the victim

Dear victory

What was done is

      UNACCEPTABLE

And

I no longer subscribe to

Or

Subject myself to

      THIS TYPE OF BEHAVIOR

Yours truly

Self Validation

LEARN

Better ways not to complain

Remember Christ and how he was tormented

When the heart is in charge

The mind plays **Second Fiddle**

And the essence of self

Gets stuck somewhere in the middle

SOMETIMES WE DO CRAZY THINGS

Loving him

Just happened to be

One of them

Beep beep beep

I still love you

Beep Beep Beep

I'll call you when I'm through

Beep Beep Beep

Let's see how long

Beep Beep Beep

You can hold your breath

Beep Beep Beep

I guess I'll see you

Beep Beep Beep

In death

SORRY LOVE

I had confused you for sorrow

ACTS OF UNKINDNESS

Are things you cannot change

Except if it's you that is unkind

THE BEST WAY

To get over any situation

Is to get into thy self

It is there

You will find the answer

I'M FILLING MY CUP

Of all that is good for me

I've grown tired

Of you drinking you see

Never pouring anything in

Allowing myself to be served ginger ale

When I know I deserve champagne

Attraction

Most of my life I was so attracted to men who were broken

Whose faults resembled my father's

I yearned to fix what was broken with them

Until I learned to heal what was broken within me

FORGIVE YOURSELF

For what

Freedom

For who

You

HEY YOU

Yes

The you

Inside of me

I'm sorry for all the things I've done

I hope you forgive me please

So that you may find

Eternal peace

THE DIFFERENCE

Between a dreamer and believer is one will die trying and the other will keep dreaming

SOMETIMES

There is

No answer or explanation

I STRUGGLED

To validate myself

Until

I began to like myself

When I removed he from my heart

I was left with what I love to do most

🚫ART

COMPROMISE

There are over 7 Billion People on the Planet

Don't waste time on someone

Who is

Unwilling

To make

Compromises

With you

If you are carrying emotional
baggage

Tread lightly

with whom

you share

intimacy

It is there

you might find

a predator

waiting

to add to your load

kidnap

your soul

and suck the life

right out of your

spirit

FREE TO BE HAPPY
FREE TO BE GENUINE
FREE TO LAUGH
FREE TO CHOOSE
FREE TO FLY
FREE TO WRITE
FREE TO SMILE
FREE TO WINK
FREE TO TASTE
FREE TO CREATE
FREE TO VIBRATE THE UNIVERSE
SAYING
HEY YOU
YES YOU
THE ONE
WHO WAS BORN IN CONFIDENCE
DON'T EVER SETTLE FOR LESS
THAN WHAT YOU GIVE
FOR THERE YOU WILL FIND FREE
AND ALL ELSE IS JUST DOM

I WEAR THE CROWN

With inherited jewels
Some that I've had to polish
With a buffing tool
As their luster lost its shine
I haven't always worn the crown
And sometimes I put it down
Forgetting it existed at all
As it was too heavy to bear
And the company I kept
Was stealing my jewels and
My crown almost disappeared into thin air
Then a voice inside said you've been fooled
Never remove your crown again
It's a gift you see
Wrapped in your values and morality
Those jewels were placed
From what's in your heart
By God from the start
So the moral of this story is:
Queens beware
If you're removing your crown
For a man in your life
He's definitely not your king and
You're damn sure not his wife

116

To All

That I may have hurt while I was unavailable

I send you love

I send you light

I send you peace

I send you grace

I send you gratitude

NAMASTE

ALWAYS REMEMBER

Unhappiness

Loves

Company

www.ingramcontent.com/pod-product-compliance
Lightning Source LLC
Chambersburg PA
CBHW021224090426
42740CB00006B/362

AVAILABLE

AVAILABLE

GINA M. SMALLWOOD
TRUE RENAISSANCE ENTERPRISE

Unavailable/Available

Printed in the United States of America

First Printing, 2018

ISBN 978-0-9993157-5-0

True Renaissance Enterprise, LLC
Grannyd@mac.com

www.TrueRenaissance.net

AS THE LOTUS FLOWER LOOKED FROM WHICH IT GREW
IT DID NOT SEE THE MUD
IT ONLY SAW A REFLECTION OF ITS BEAUTY

THIS BOOK IS DEDICATED
TO MY LATE SON KELVIN MIKHAIL
WHO WILL ALWAYS BE THE LOTUS OF MY LIFE

CONTENTS

CONTENTS

CONTENTS

Life does not always offer exemptions of hardships based on the goodness of what's in a person's heart!
What life does offer, however, is a choice to thrive in kindness and inspire others to do the same no matter the circumstance.

Preface

This is a story about a woman whose fear was turned into love, whose pain was turned into joy, and whose traumatic experiences were released so that she could have space for peace. After having suffered much abuse and trauma (from physical beatings, emotional and sexual assault, a loaded shotgun to her face, the transition of her only child to suicide and her only sibling to cancer, finding her father's decomposed body, and the many (sometimes sudden) transitions of other loved ones) God pushed her past surviving into thriving. With it came the gift of acceptance and the knowledge that everything has a polar opposite and somewhere in between is truth! The truth to be present and not to take life's experiences personal.

It had been 40 years she suffered with her norms of incomprehensible pain, sometimes stinging others along the way, so that they could feel the depths of her turmoil. Even after her son's death, she did not allow herself to fully process the pain. Instead she turned into a ghost so that she could feed other willing hosts. After all she had become accustomed to learned behavior of being hard and judgmental, especially with herself. She had learned to compress trauma at the young age of one when her father was shot and completely blinded. With it, her innocence was lost and she became eyes to her father's brilliance and his tormented psyche.

This all became clear one day, as she continued to struggle years after her son's transition, she noticed from a distance a young girl around the age of five walking hand in hand with her father and the picturesque portrayal of innocence. It was as if the fog in her life removed itself at that very moment. She had not had that experience and it was for what she longed. What became even clearer was all of the words of endearment expressed over the years from people who loved her, how she never felt love because she was stuck in pain. Not until that very moment did she realize she could pick up all the sharp edges of her life without fearing cuts because she owed it to herself, and yes she knew she had to be brave and yes she knew she had to be strong.

11

The strength she attributes to God who has never left her, not even in the darkest loneliest hours. Her undying faith in the omnipresence of God's existence is a reminder that there is a beginning and end to everything, even suffering. As she begins to process her emotions of fear and pain with being unavailable, she cleared up space so she could be available. This is Herstory in poetry, prose, quotes and letters of healing, allowing all the necessary time to process her suffering, and learning to love herself, so that she could experience more joy and live fully in peace. Hallelujah!

Acknowledgements

To God Be the Glory! Even God knows humans need medical and mental health doctors, and boy was I in dire need of great mental health practitioner. It took years to locate a therapist who could deal with all the trauma and drama. The therapist I sought earlier in my life were to help with issues in the 14 year marriage that ended in divorce. Years later one of the therapist I went to after my son's transition started crying during the first session and that would also be the last session with that therapist.

Then I did some research and found Dr. Rona Fields, who cracked open my hard existence like an egg allowing my entire yolk to spill. I had finally met my match! She was special, and dedicated her life to doing research and studying trauma all over the world. Her final book "Against Violence Against Women – The Case for Gender as a Protected Class" goes into the depths of just how long women have been the target for violence and why. Because Dr. Fields had courage to unmask the world, she unmasked me within a matter of months, she gave me tools to empower myself, and the change became evident to all who know and love me. I am a better person because of her dedication to mental health.

In the midst of when I was just beginning to share my deepest pain, as it related to my father, my father transitioned and so did Dr. Fields. It was then I realized, Dr. Fields had taught me everything I needed to cope in life, she restored my innocence and I wanted to make sure I acknowledged her and all of her hard work in making this world a better place.

Although, I had already begin writing this book, I never got to share it with her, but I do know she and all the other people I love who have transitioned are smiling with me. My hopes are that this book be a useful tool for people who are experiencing unbearable pain to get the help they may need to experience more love, more joy and more peace. This is not a replacement for appropriate professional help, but definitely a useful tool for self-help.

I also would like to acknowledge my mother who has allowed my whimsical wildflower spirit to be free and has always dedicated herself to her family. To my Madrina Aida and my Aunt Judy, thanks for letting me entertain you with my stories that bring you laughter. Thanks to my nieces Sydney, Ashley, and Chanel who stepped in to support me like their mother, my late sister Lydia, would have through this process.

To all my great and beautiful family, mentees, mentors, and friends, I would like to acknowledge all the ways you loved me even when I could not feel your love. You all are rockstars and I'm glad I am still here to show and tell you.

Many blessings to my friend, Annie, who shared her love for the earth and taught me so much about its healing power. To my cousin Sunny, thanks for recording your voice, and your spirit has been a calm through many storms. To my cousin Tonya for always reminding me Art is life and everything else is an illusion. To Monica for being the best Godmother to Mick! To Lori and Brigette for being my dearest and best friends. To Bethany and Remone for being like my siblings and children all in one.

Jimmy, you get the Oscar, your undying love and dedication since Kelvin's transition is worthy of a seat on on the right hand side of Jesus. You are living proof that there is good in the world and I am forever grateful to you, son!

Special thanks to my editor, G.L. Morrison, your clarifying comments, your patience, your bravery in continuing to read some of the unavailable pieces that are raw and most of all for connecting as a woman, a mother, a wife, and a genuine person. Your openness and support made the process of finalizing this book a reality and I am forever grateful!

Gina M. Smallwood
Sacred Moon Life Center, Georgia 04/28/18

About the AuthOr

Gina M. Smallwood, a University of Maryland University College graduate, is an Accountant, Artist and Activist who operates a healing space called Sacred Moon Life Center in Georgia. As an Accountant she is a contractor for not-for-profit and government entities. She also Chairs the Kelvin Mikhail Suicide Awareness Campaign in tribute to her late son Kelvin who died in 2008 from suicide. As part of the campaign she delivers workshops and also trains people in Mental Health First Aid. As an Artist, she loves architectural design and creates stained glass art pieces and other industrial art for homes. She is also trained as a mediator in the state of Georgia, a professional coach and spiritual advisor. Gina loves to travel to exotic places and incorporate her rare finds into schematic themes. For more information, please visit: www.TrueRenaissance.net

Lost in the Hood

I found her
Just when I stopped looking
She was right there
Where I left her years ago
Free of
Self-hatred
Neglect
Rejection
Submission
Full of
Beauty
Transparency
Love
Joy
Peace
Yep
I found her
And this little red riding Ain't lost in the Hood no more!

Available

Is what I choose to Be
A woman of strength
A woman of courage
A woman of conviction
A woman in my own skin
I am every woman
I am every daughter
I am every sister
I am every mother
The womb
The life
The teacher
The nurturer
The lover
The friend
The wife
The spirit of water within

No more tears of pain
No more victim in my veins
Hear my spell in the wishing well
I am wise
Here's the door to vulnerability inside
Meet my true friend
My heart
Authentic being
The core wrapped in a body of meaning
Hear me roar
Sounds beat
Vibrations
Currents of the ocean and the sea
I am unapologetically me
Wind underneath my wings and on my back
I am available to love
I am available to experience joy and
I am available to live in peace

CHAPTER ONE - LOVE

L etting

O bstacles

V anish

E ntirely

The Ultimate Chapter

Love yourself

through the pain
Love yourself
you stand a lot to gain
Love yourself
you are strength.
Love yourself
no more imaginary
ifs
ands
or
buts
The truth is
your love
has
is
and always
been enough

The Crown

And I picked her up
The crown that is
The one I was born to wear
Although dusty
She had been through hell and back
As I polished each stone to its splendor
I begin to see a reflection of me
The true love of self
I always wanted to be

Love...

Could Love simply be
Light
Cheer
Laughter
The reflection of all the goodness
Your heart desires in the hereafter

LIKE THE BLOOMS IN THE GARDEN OF RHODODENDRONS

I see her face
Bright smile
Through the thick leaves
A flower composed with many clusters
Daughter
Mother
Wife
Friend
Standing and holding
Grounded
Nothing impacts the beauty of this flower
Not even
The rain
Clouds
Or wind
She's made
Her way through darkness
Spreading light with colors
Hues of purple white and pink
Sharing her fragrance once again
In our hearts she will always be

The Greatest

Acts of love one can experience are

A smile

A hug

A tender touch

That same love reflected back to us

Just a Dream

I tasted you last night in a vivid dream
It was a little different as your complexion was that of
cream
Somehow I met you near the water
You took me out to sea
Courting me in just one day
Sharing your love for life with me
We poured over places you traveled
And how water journeys had brought you peace
You reached over kindly, slowly placed your lips
Kissing me gently as the sun began to set
The taste of you unfamiliar
Yet deliciously heaven sent
When we landed on dry land
You began to express more interest in me
Somehow the need to meet my entire family
Shook me to the core
Abruptly awakening me
Leaving me wanting you more
I remember you as my prelude to love
A coming attraction
With my eyes open wide
I smile knowing you are there
Somewhere waiting to love me
Until then
My heart is open with a place for thee
Beating rhythms of a drum waiting patiently
Until this is reality and no longer just a dream

Seconds per day

THERE ARE 86,400 SECONDS PER DAY

I'M CHOOSING ALL OF THOSE

SECONDS TO LOVE

 AND BE LOVE

START YOUR DAY
WITH LOVE

End your day with love

Run

To some familiar place
Trying not to get lost
In the same chase
Heavy
Tired
Lonesome road
Leading me back
Overload
I don't have to go

Run

Over and over
Where this time
Jumping over hurdles
Of the past
Finally taking with me
Love at last

Run

Finding meaning
To my life
Facing challenges as they come and go
Humility
Sharing only the smile upon this beautiful face

Run

To the Lord
Slowing it down
Taking in a new breath
Hold my hand
Hold my hand
Guide me through
I don't ever want to run
And miss being with you

Run

As I close my eyes
With the knowledge
I no longer have to keep up a pace
And nothing in this life is ever left undone
I'm learning to listen
Carefully to what's inside
Before I take another stride
Missing the stillness of grace
Placed upon me
Let's me know the only run is with thee

Dear Daddy,

Thank you for sharing your love of music and your love of dance.

Thank you for teaching me *"God bless the child who has their own"* and to be independent.

Thank you for teaching me that worrying is a sin and
to be patient or become one.

Most importantly:
Thank you for teaching me to trust God for everything. Through your indiscretions, I learned to know God more intimately.

The old saying
"Looking for love in all the wrong places"

Stop looking

Be still

Feel

It is right here

It's been here all the time

Patiently waiting

Your arrival

As he manifests in my heart
So does the love of the sea
Reaching to the horizon of the moon
He respects the womb
His passage into existence is through
The tears that flow come not from pain
But from the joy of God's creation
The smile
He sees my heart
It's pure
It's vast
It's deep
It takes flight
It weathers storms
It sees beauty in everything
It knows peace
It knows that stillness comes and glows
As the breath is rare
So is the pulse of the beat
Suspended in thin air
Walking this earth
Landing on feet

We Meet

Most-simple

The most-simple act of love resides in a smile

High in the hills of a familiar place

There's a **Treasure** buried deep

It takes nothing to give away

But it can take everything to accept

It is not bold or boastful

It is not impatient or unkind

It sits and waits patiently

To blanket

It is truly divine

When it captures a being

It can never be outdone

It does not compete

Or form any kind of shame

It fluently

Speaks every seeker's name

Sometimes it whispers

With grace to bestow

Leaving all enlightened

With a special glow

Love is the language of the heart

It is the supernatural frame of art

Love is

Something you give

But

You cannot take back

It remains

When you remove
the you and I
out or away from love
Love is still there
It remains

Whether
we
you
I
are a part of love
It remains

Just as the sky
the moon
the sun
the flower blooms

It -that thing called love- remains

Love Does Not
Have strings

To the Moon and Back

I love you
Made from the same thread
Intertwined from the beginning
There will never be an ending
Brief breaks of independence
Vast liberties of extension
Fluid as a raindrop
Turned into a sea
The ripples
This emotion carries will always be with me

To the Moon
I would go
Even out into space
There could never be anyone to take your place
Light years in time
Could not even disconnect
How much I love you
Just as the sky is blue
When I look in the mirror
I will always see reflections of you

And back

And forth

Without a clue
The traces of our existence
Will always be true

Even though the measurement
Of the moon to the earth
Round trip
Is 480 thousand miles
I would gladly carry you on my back
Embracing that distance with a smile

The phrase became our expression during your final months
A journey
Only a sibling might take
Branded in my heart
Knowing as sisters
We love to the moon and back

Speak to me of Love

And God Spoke

Speak to you of Love my Child

For what You Possess

Is what you will receive in return

Reflection

Smiles every time I see a reflection of
myself in your face

A brand new day bright and sunny

filled with joy

A heartbeat with the rhythm of one

Every day with laughter and fun

Moonlight found in each other's eyes

Peace so still

we speak to each other's thoughts

For we are one

Yoked with God and love

Here on earth and heavenly bound

The more I love

The better I become with hello

JUST YOU JUST ME

Love does exist in you in me

And when we look at each other

We can see

The abundance of serenity

When we hold each other's hands and dance cheek to
cheek

The splendor of love is complete

Tasting what we prepare together

Feeding each other's souls,

We learn there has never been a need to control

For our love is not boastful and needs no explanation

It's just you

It's just me

Sharing love's ecstasy

I know love like the clouds know the rain

Dropping in my heart without any fear or pain

For love dwells in the kindest of men

Keeping their souls far away from sin

I want to taste it in this lifetime

Like it's coffee with cream

Bright as the northern star

Twinkle Twinkle

I'll wait patiently

For I know it is not very far

To Know Love

I must embrace love
I must confess love
Oneness with God completes my love
Planted like the seed love
The fruit I bear love
Leaving me in suspended air love
For the love I seek is pure as it resides in my
heart
Love only adds, it doesn't subtract
It gives sentiments of gratefulness every day love
Love has no limit
No denominator to tow love
I see you my love
I feel you my love
You are love
My love

Acts of Kindness

Are the light of love

LOVE HAS A NEW NAME

And Spirit Spoke:

The feeling of delight
Out of sight
Can you dig
Deeper than you know

Love Has a New Name

Multiply the high
No division
Just sky
Blue, red, purple, grey, orange, yellow, every hue

Love Has a New Name

Splendor
Are you a vendor?
Drown me
Let the cup runneth over
Lost in it

Love Has a New Name

Tell tales
Spread the word
Like the roots of the largest tree
Without a forest

Love Has a New Name

Cover you
Cover me
In light
Expanding spirit
Take flight

Love Has a New Name

Birth it
Live it
Cherish it
Succumb to it
Resonate in it
Be still in it
Know it
Carry it
Share it

Love Has a New Name
And that Name is You

WHERE Love DWELLS

THERE IS NO ROOM FOR HATE

Dear Womb

I never knew such love until
You housed a seed
Allowing it to grow
Giving birth to a beautiful life
An amazing son
A humble soul

A Lovely Spirit

Such a lovely spirit is he

Feeling people's hearts is his great legacy

One by One he shared himself

Not asking for much

Always giving even the slightest touch

His possession of stillness could almost say it all

This young man was like a melody to a song

Before his time

Deeper than we know

For in his greatness he had to go

His time here on earth in the physical was so well
spent

That God knew when he shared this young man

His purpose of love would forever be felt

Dear Mick,

Happy Birthday! 26 years ago, God bestowed a gift, the joy of life. I love you always and I'm really sorry that I didn't see your pain, as the joy of who you are outshined it.

I do have to let you know that your existence touched many lives, some in a profound way. My birthday wish for you today and always is that of Love and that everyone whose life you touched gains a better understanding that you didn't chose mental pain. That your life was not in vain and many lives have been saved because you lived.

Albeit having you here physically to see what you would be contributing to the universe remains a dream that all who love you continue to live out for you. May you Rest In Peace, my beautiful, amazing, brilliant, wise, one and only birth son.

Peace, Ma

YOU ARE LOVE

If you don't know that yet
and are stuck
May I suggest you flip this book

I'M LOOKING FOR AN OLD G

Someone who's got a heart like me
Not playing the field
'Cause his desire is in a wildflower
Mature in what he wants
He is not a broke down brother
A legacy
Established enough for seven generations
He's an old G you see
He's a man
Not a boy
Looking for a toy to bring him joy
He knows academia
Like he knows the streets
He's an old G you see
Confident
Swagger in his style
Well-traveled brother
Dynamic In his stride
Breaking down any situation when he talks
He ain't trippin off of nothing
He already knows the walk
This brother got it going on
He's an old G you see
It's in his smile
And
This girl knows it
'Cause what's in her heart has been there for a while
And she desires the caliber of a man
That's an old G you see

Love Is Not Something
You Can Find

Nor can you look for it

When you love you
You love completely

Love from something or someone else is a
compliment
A reflection

Not something sought and found

And

Once you know love
Nothing else really matters

My love is …

Kind
Exceptional
Rare
Inspirational
Beautiful
Deep
Life Changing
Spiritual
Ready
Righteous
Strength
Worthy
Bright as the Sun
Bright as the Moon
Vast as the Sky
Unconditional

Love

My Deepest Love

Can I share with you my secrets

For you and I are the only ones who need to know

Can I keep you with me throughout eternity

For the love I feel for you is deeper than a mother's love for her child

Can I go with you to see the light

For the emptiness I would feel without you

is deeper than I would ever know

Can I, God

God the creator who art everywhere with and in
everything, we are you

Hallowed be thy name

Thy light shines in all

 Gifting with it peace

 Found in the heart not in the mind

May this truth soon fill all empty space

For the darkness that looms in the waking hour is
that of the dead

Give us this day our daily bread, our daily light

To remove all shadows of hopelessness and doubt

Remind us that there is no separation

So that we may forgive ourselves

Just as you forgive us

May we accept that darkness comes with night

And having you in our hearts at all times is the
light

And the salvation that removes all temptation
from sight

God

 All one

 One love

Then Love Appeared ...

Stone
(1)

Hold me dear

As if I were here

Let me penetrate your soul

Imagine all that is in me

Is right next to you

Bringing you comfort while you sleep

For in the morning when you wake

And you find yourself temporarily alone

Remember the love I feel for you

Is written in Stone

Repeat
(2)

As I gaze into your eyes

Before I slumber

I can't think of any other

I'd rather have this exchange

For this type of love

Comes straight from above

So powerful and sweet

I can't wait for nightfall to repeat

Lucky Charm
(3)

I lay next to you

With open arms

Waiting to squeeze and hold you

Like a lucky charm

I find comfort in your warmth

Your smell

Your soft touch

Smooth as silk

I love you so much

Holding You
(4)

When I woke

I begin to prepare you for our next encounter

As I started to anticipate the next time we would cuddle

My eyes went into a trance

My heart skipped a beat

I begin to dance

Thinking about our next romance

Surely you feel the same way

As you winked and smiled

Acknowledging too would be a long day

Until I get back

My thoughts will be holding you

Naturally
(5)

Thanks for bringing me comfort

Morning, noon and night

The joy you give is always right

Perfection is all over your face

When I lay my head down

There's always grace

Asleep in your arms is where I like to be

And with you it comes so naturally

Only You
(6)

I can go deeper with you than anyone else

To a shallow breath

Sometimes I can't help myself

You surround me in unimaginable ways

As I begin to fall asleep

Rays of color

So rare in detail

As I reach out to squeeze you

You remain in my arms

I continue in this beautiful nightly song

Dreaming of only you

Ecstasy
(7)

Skin smooth

Soft as butter

You make my heart flutter

I see stars in your eyes

The taste of your kiss

Always leaves me mesmerized

Pulling you close

Having you next to me

Keeps my spirit in ecstasy

Dreams
(8)

When you breathe

I breathe

When you smile

I smile

Soft to the touch

I love you so much

Can't think of a place

I would rather be

Than lying next to you

And having wonderful dreams

Lifetime
(9)

When I slumber

I only think of you

Sometimes I lay awake

Watching you sleep

Trying to get a glimpse of

What's come over me

Every part of your being

Resonates with mine

Letting me know

What we have is for a lifetime

About You
(10)

I'm in total bliss

Everytime we kiss

The sweet scent that covers you

Resonates with me

Leaving me wanting more

As I go through the day

I anticipate our next encounter

My total existence comes to a halt

Because all I can think about is you

Higher Ground
(11)

Before I close my eyes at night
My thoughts go straight to holding you tight
Your tenderness reminds me of how much I'm blessed
Let it be you and me
Always
My best friend
My love
My destiny
The connection that we share
Is safe and sound
And keeps me rooted on higher ground

Absolute
(12)

When I wake all I see is you
In bold colors
Our love is true
You astound me with purity
That warms my heart
Shaping and penetrating every part
Each day I find myself never wandering
Only thoughts of you
This desired feel is a reminder
You my sweet
are the absolute truth

Twelve Slumbers later

It suddenly was clear
The love that appeared
was simply

In a pillow…

CHAPTER TWO - JOY

J ustifiable

O ptimistic

Y ou

The Everyday Chapter

I learned to enjoy my own company...

Now I cannot get enough of it

Herein lies my Joy:

Communing with nature in the morning

Dancing til my clothes are wet

Laughing at myself

Writing profound words

Birthing art

Traveling to exotic international places

Watching the moon and movies

Sleeping at least 6 hours of uninterrupted sleep

Helping people to think outside the box

Cooking orgasmic meals

Swimming with dolphins and whale sharks

Singing off key out loud

Having deep conversations

Talking to babies toddlers and children

Gardening

Reading spiritual books

Going to museums and vineyards

Shopping at thrift stores and finding rare items

Hanging with friends

Loving my life and doing what's in my heart

And what is your joy
Write it ...

Breath it

Embrace it

Spread it

Nurture it

Ride it

Smile with it

Let it resonate in unimaginable ways

Different Realities

Life offers many different realities

Perhaps if we looked at these experiences

 as just a glimpse

Then the trials and tribulations

Merely become a road to heighten

Our positive experiences

Bringing less pain

Creating more joy

In joy

Every experience has no expectations

It is when expectations are placed

The sight of joy is lost and we cease to exist

It's in the air

Spreading hope everywhere

It can calm and

Silence pain

It is present even in the rain

It is free for all to receive

And it isn't found in any material gain

Joy comes in the morning

Although you may not feel it at night

When you wake with another day to experience it

It is pure delight

Life can be full of disappointment

If you rely on other people to bring you joy

How about you be joy

And bring it into everything

You **think**

You **say**

And

You **do**

Juicy Ass Jamaican sky

Damn

What just happened
I let myself go
Face off
Say it ain't so
No kissing
No licky-licky please
Just dive right in
The queen wants
To play with the king
Penetration

Damn

That shit felt good
Lucid and wet
Ready to ride that
Jamaican
New York born
Chocolate Wood
Caramel
Sweet

Damn

Here comes the sun
Where we flying to
That's the lure
The trap
I can't get caught up
In none of that
This shit is sexy fun
Not enough time to repeat

Damn

To the States I must return
To play hard
Get what I want
Creating
The illusion
Red carpet
Plane rides
Yachts
Swimming naked
Pure serenity
The sun
The moon
The sea

And that Juicy ass Jamaican sky

Joy Inside

Make it become an intricate part
of your being until it reaches
every cell in your body
Sprinkle it like the wind and dust
until that joy inside
covers the entire universe

Touched

From the second you entered my world
I knew that I was blessed
With this beautiful spark
Sent directly from God above
Removing the fear that I was somehow unprepared
To nurture a spirit greater than myself
As I carried you in the womb listening to music and
Reading you books
Fine-tuning you into to your earthly wings
I had no idea the joy you would bring
As I marveled at some of the things you did
I was so fortunate to know you were my kid
As time passed and I saw you grow
The choices you made for yourself let me know
You were a Prince of Peace filled with love
When the world seemed so bleak
I remember many times I wanted to protect you
I knew you were a jewel
You stood your ground letting me know
You were a young man and I could let you go
Reminding me the protection that I sought was in God's hands
Character, my son, was your greatest strength
For in it you lead many to know that hard work pays off and Our
reason for existence is to love with all our heart
And on a continuum to always be kind
Since your transition, it's been hard for me to know
I'll never be able to hear your voice, your laughter your pokes,
your kiss, but every part of your existence
brought me joy and has left me touched

NOTHING
LIKE
THE JOY
OF
BEING
A MOTHER

I am a derivative of love
There is no greater emotion than me
I bring out happiness
I can fill an empty space
Although sometimes I'm forgotten
Except in names and holiday cards
When I'm felt
I fill a room
It is what I like to do
Spreading myself thick and wide
Covering eyes
Opening hearts
Contagious
I am the mend to life
If you are experiencing me daily
Then you already know who I am
And when you wake to a new day
I hope it is me you see again and again

Joy

No one can steal it

Your joy

or

Your happiness

Only you can give it away

The Spirit that is Joy

Is

The Spirit that is Holy

Encircled with the enrichment of being

To give of love
In its silence
*Is the **Whisper** of Joy*

Put a dollar in a jar
Every time you experience joy
You may just end up
a **Millionaire**

It has been a joy

Sharing parts of me with you

Every morning when you rise
Know that there is Joy in your eyes
If you can't find it
May I Suggest
You go back to sleep and repeat

Tis your life

Forget about tis the season to be jolly

Tis your life to have joy

Because I do…

Because it's beautiful…

Because it is what life is all about…

That Experience of Joy

To Dance

Is to know Joy

It is there in the rhythm

and the beat

That the heart and
Spirit are free

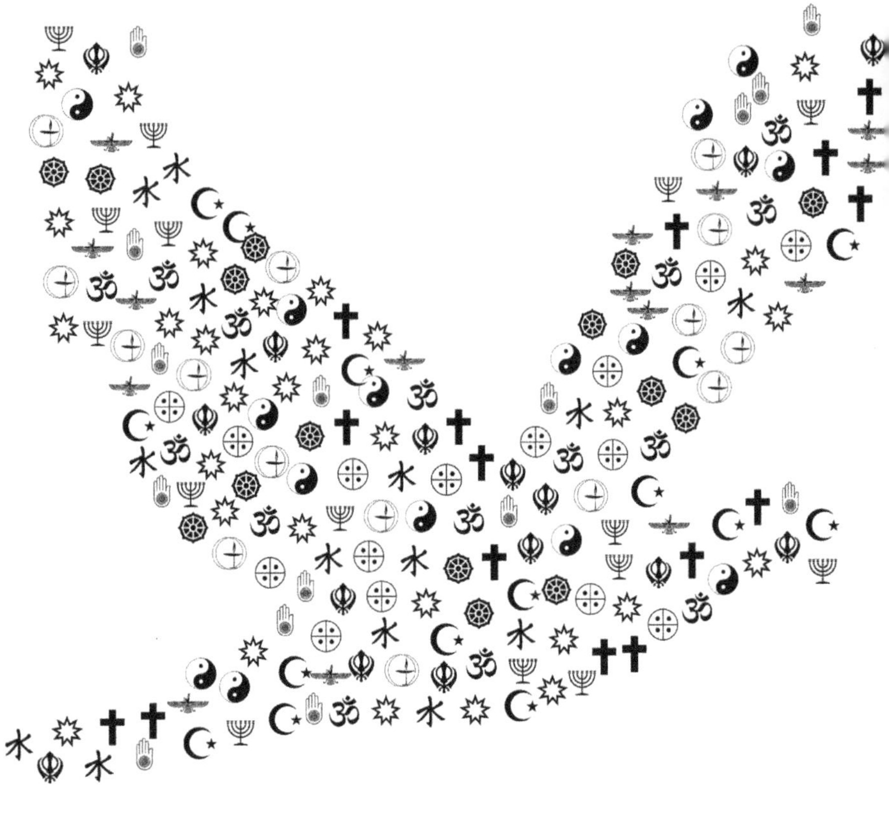

CHAPTER THREE - PEACE

Please

Excuse

Accept

Consider

Everything

The Final Chapter

Lost and Found

I walked around with my feelings on my shoulder

My skin was as thin as air

Every comment I took personal

Letting other people's perceptions define me

I was so lost having no boundaries

Turmoil became my norm

That was until Peace found me

Wrapping me

With reassurance

Grabbing my total being

Letting me see truth

There is no need for explanation

Meaning or clue

No worry

Others will see me through you

I am eternally embedded in everything you do

The strength of your shoulders is now my weight

Your skin is thickened as I give you grace

Comments are just symbols other people use

Sometimes with no meaning especially if they are confused

I want you to share me through every single breath

Until I become the norm

And the universe no longer feels turmoil or stress

In the eye of any storm is where you'll find it

Peace that is

The easiest way to peace is to understand

Someone else's right

Does not mean someone else is wrong

Peace is the revolution

Live in it

Let it live in you

L.I.P.

There is PEACE in knowing you may
go through hell...

But all will end well

IF YOU HAVE A PROBLEM WITH SOMEONE ELSE....

TAKE A LOOK AT YOURSELF

The one truth:

Breathe

That of the wave…

Renews me
With each splash
Cleanse
Purify my existence
Move me to greener pastures
Splash
As the wind pushes
Bringing with it change
Alternate
Smooth
Splash
Rolling
It's the earth moving
Shallow waters
Taking breath
Leaving evidence
Remarkable rock
Turned to sand
Taking with it
That which it gave
Water and Wind

Simply PEACEFUL and that of a Wave

Peace is to **Transform** all that is painful
to accepting life's imperfections

Freedom

Live from the heart and
Out loud

But remember …

Not everyone knows that same freedom

Piece of Peace

It is a clear day for all to see
The power and the glory bestowed on thee
Times are rough
Seek the road less traveled
Carry through
There is storm of strength inside of you
In the eye is where there is light

Equilibrium
Take flight
Watch a bird
Balance its wings
Breathing air
One of life's most simple things

Slow down
Hurrying is the past
The sentiments of its destruction
Fulfilled with pain and disappointment
Future expectations aren't realized
No longer brings

Yet, does not materialize on it's own
Grace is a gift written in stone
Given to all mankind to find the way
To freedom liberty and justice for all
Is the resurrection of the fall

Join forces to become one
Connecting to what is in the heart
Passion for kindness is the start
Forgiveness is connected to lack
This is no longer part of the track

Humanitarianism is what we take back
Keeping it in the forefront of change
Bringing nuances that ring

Mercy the common ground for which we stand
Aligns our energy to become one
Opening the floodgates of love
Giving insight to nothing left undone

As we wake to that new day
Finding our contribution
The reflection, the constitution
A mirror that we all are

A piece of universal peace

Peace is

Taking one moment at a time
With patience and kindness
In every
Thought
Word
and Action

God doesn't punish

We do that all by ourselves

Sabotaging

If you are taking life personal

You are sabotaging your peace

PRAY

MEDITATE

LIVE

FOR

PEACE

To be still with your thoughts

Is to **Know Peace**

THROUGH GOD'S GRACE
WE ARE GIFTED FREE WILL TO CHOOSE

THAT OF CHAOS
OR
THAT OF PEACE

I choose Peace

Where's your peace

WHEN ONE PERSON EXPERIENCES PEACE

WE ALL EXPERIENCE IT

FIND IT

Peace that is

And

Never let it go

Peace is when your heart tells your mind

"I Got This"

Because I can…

Because I choose to…

Because I want to…

Be Peace

Hold on to Nothing,
It is there you will find Peace!

Peace is when you realize everything in life is temporary

Except……

The love that bears your name

You are Me
And
I am you

When I live in peace
You do too

Be the peace that lives in me
And
I will be the peace that lives in you

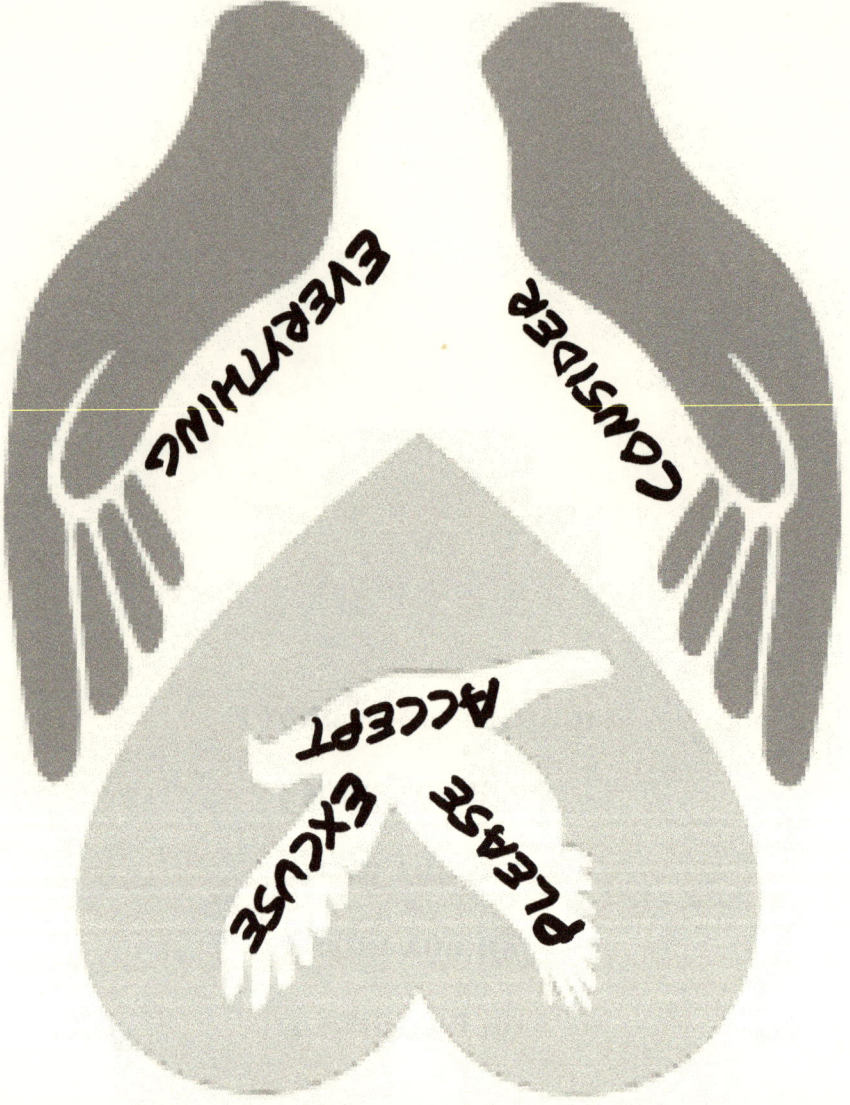

CONSIDER EVERYTHING

PLEASE EXCUSE ACCEPT

TO THE UNIVERSE AND ALL OF ITS INHABITANTS

I send you love

I send you light

I send you peace

I send you grace

I send you Gratitude

NAMASTE

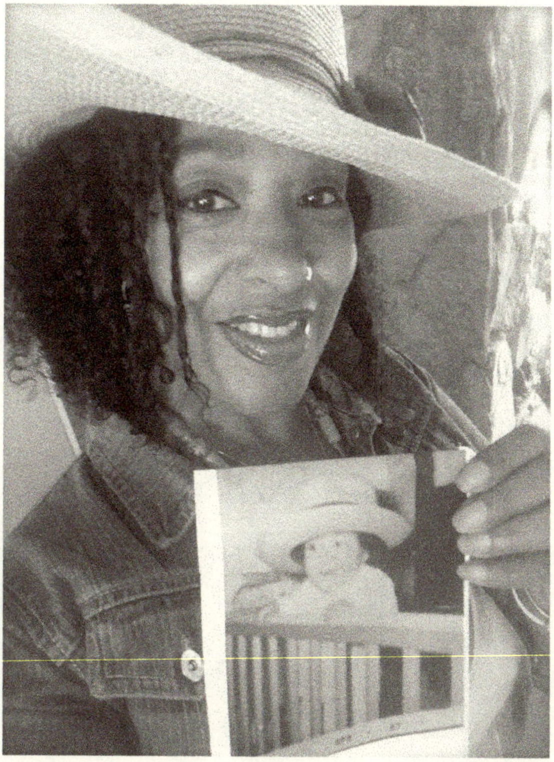

Always Know

Happiness is…
Its own Company